LIVING HISTORY

A Guide to Reconstructing the Past with Children

by

John Fairclough and Patrick Redsell

PREFACE

Putting children into a living reconstruction of the past enables them to learn by experiencing a totally different way of life and at the same time to acquire a greater interest in our heritage as represented by historic buildings. It makes it easier to teach them what it felt like to live in the past—something that is very difficult to convey in the classroom or even during the usual type of visit to a historic site.

If we want pupils to understand why people acted as they did, we must introduce them to a broader community of people and events than the usual simplified school version of history in which complex evidence is reduced to a short series of events so that the Normans come to mean simply Conquest, Castles and Barons. This hardly begins to use the range of evidence which would give a clearer idea of what life was like. Much of that evidence can be incorporated into the type of living history project described here. While the actual day of the visit to the project is a much more profound experience than the average school visit to an historic building, it is also the focus for a deeper study than is usually possible of one part of the past. Preparation to take part in the project provides the stimulus for a class to study a particular historical period in more depth and apply historical skills intensively to one moment in the past.

This approach to history provides a technique of simulation for teachers themselves to use at historic sites throughout the country or in their own schools and local environments.

Montagu of Beaulieu

Lord Montague of Beaulieu
Chairman of English Heritage

CONTENTS

INTRODUCTION

This introduction to the use of dramatic reconstructions in helping children to learn about the past is based on the authors' experience of organising projects in Suffolk since 1978.

Our first collaboration was called *Fire at Cranley Green*. A team of local amateur actors visited schools in Suffolk to work with classes to recreate the story of a rick burning in the area during the 1840s. The children were divided into groups each led by an actor, then took on the roles of the people involved, discussing the reasons for their behaviour and actions. Often this work took place out of doors in the fields and among farm buildings of the nineteenth century. In this way a particular local historical event was used to explore important issues of social history. To extend the children's knowledge of the nineteenth century, teachers were able to borrow a set of objects of the period from the museum service, together with a pack of reproductions of contemporary documents—newspaper articles, bills of sale, transcripts of court cases. This gave *them* the opportunity to examine some of the evidence on which the recreation was based.

The drama team had also been involved in a number of one day fairs, in which children from many schools worked with their teachers to recreate the events and the atmosphere of a Suffolk fair in a previous century. They produced objects and entertainments using traditional techniques and materials. These events took place in a local park under the heading *Midsummer 1553* or *Midsummer 1853*. Everyone taking part wore the clothes of the period, and a number of amateur actors took on the roles of people who lived at the time, roles they held throughout the length of the fair, so that the children taking part experienced something of the social attitudes of people who lived then.

After these initial explorations of the use of drama to achieve greater understanding of the past, we set about a large scale historical reconstruction. The focus for this was Heveningham Hall, a Georgian country house that was little changed from its condition in the last decade of the eighteenth century. With the support of the Department of the Environment who then owned the house and the National Trust who administered it, every day for a week we could bring the house back to life as it was in the summer of 1790, by introducing two hundred pupils as estate workers. Our aim was that children should learn about a particular aspect of history through experiencing it for themselves, working as participants in the events and not just as observers. Building upon our previous experience, we added to this the use of teachers in role.

It was important to us that this reconstruction was created from local resources, that it was a cooperative venture between schools, teachers and the local community. *Heveningham Hall, Midsummer 1790* was organised for a second year in 1980.

In 1981, with help from the Department of the Environment we took a similar approach to the reconstruction of medieval life in and around the castles of Framlingham and Orford, (*Bigod's Suffolk 1173*). For two weeks, one hundred and fifty children each day worked in an encampment in the castle grounds. After an introductory assembly in the twelfth century stone keep, they became apprentices, constructing the outer defences of the castle in anticipation of a siege. In the past few years this work has been centred on the coastal castle at Orford.

After talking to many different audiences about these reconstructions we have brought together in this publication the results of our experience in the belief that others can apply the ideas in different locations to meet their particular needs. In the following pages we combine an account of our projects with suggestions that can be used in other places, and an explanation of the philosophy behind the ideas.

CHOOSING THE LOCATION

In order to provide a worthwhile experience, it is vital that the total setting of the reconstruction should be as accurate as possible. This is greatly helped by using a building of the period you wish to study, as in the case of our Georgian country house or a medieval castle. Not only do they provide the right physical surroundings, but it also helps to be recreating the events of the past in the place where they actually took place. At the same time we are bringing the building itself to life. Often when schools visit a great house or ancient monument it appears dead because however well it is cared for and displayed, the way of life that gave it meaning has gone, it lacks the people who kept it alive. Working with quite large numbers of children at a time and guiding them in suitable tasks, it is possible to people these monuments with the sort of numbers that made them busy centres of importance. There can be little doubt that children learn more about life in the building if they have to work in it rather than if they just look at it as outsiders.

Heveningham Hall is an imposing 18th century house set deep in the countryside of mid Suffolk. The local road swings a corner out of woods to reveal a reed encircled lake from which rises a slope of pasture and grazing sheep. At the head of the slope stands the house, rectangular, neo classical in design and constructed in blocks of cream coloured stone on three floors. The approach road leads to a circular courtyard containing stables and workshops, while in the sheltered lee of the house are walled formal gardens, beyond which are the landscaped and wooded grounds of the estate. Half a mile away but placed discreetly out of sight from the hall is the village of Huntingfield, once a place of residence for the estate workers. During the eighteenth and nineteenth centuries the house, its gardens and grounds as well as the local farms and villages must have provided life, work and community for many people. Children who visit the house today to walk around the echoing rooms and carefully tended gardens would have little understanding of the way the community existed and was sustained. They could have only a fleeting impression of the look and feel of a previous age, of the way people behaved towards each other, of the work they did, of the food they ate, the conditions they lived under, of the things they said to each other, the values they held. At the same time, the evidence— in writing, music, illustrations, objects is there, but seldom in a form which children can approach. But a knowledge of all these things, a capacity to make sense of the evidence is what we try to lead

children towards. An imaginative grasp and understanding of Who? How? Where? are the means by which we can relate what we see and do now, in the present, to what they saw and did in the past. The line of development is uncovered and illuminated. *Then* and *Now* are connected.

Our aim became to set up a reconstruction of 1790 at Heveningham Hall, using as much evidence and information as we could find, and then provide the opportunity for children between the ages of 9 and 13 to experience directly the life and events of the past. It was not to be a Pageant in which the children were spectators, nor the indulgence of adults in costume being attended by children in a great pantomime. Throughout, the questions we asked were: *What will the children discover and learn?* and *How will we know what they have learned?* In other words, at the centre of our thinking was the child as participant, learning through direct experience.

The existence of the Hall and our access to some of the rooms in it, as well as to the grounds, pointed to the idea of inviting children to work at the Hall as if it was a day in the past. They were to be the people who kept the house running by cooking, gardening, building and repairing, not just the stereotype servant in frock coat and white gloves bowing and scraping before the bewigged gentry. The emphasis was to be on methods and techniques. The children were to be the estate workers, as far as possible using the tools and equipment which would have been in use in the summer of 1790. Water would be drawn from a well and carried, not taken from the taps. Meals were to be cooked on a range, rush lights and candles were to be prepared for the onset of darkness. Everyone was to wear the clothes of the past. The way we organised the working groups and the tasks they each undertook gave the children an understanding of how different life was without many of the things we take for granted now, but we were equally concerned to give a clearer idea of social organisation and attitudes of the time.

It occurred to us that an eighteenth century owner and his family in residence could provide that. The Vanneck family appeared in our plans. A group of actors from the Wolsey Theatre at Ipswich would take on the roles of the family for the day. They would pass their day in the house and about the grounds, expect their needs to be met diligently and discreetly by their family of estate workers. Sir Joshua, his wife and children would tour and visit the estate, give a benevolent ear to cases of hardship, and inspect work in progress. Their day would be an ordinary one. The profile of their presence would be modest though powerful. They would not give a performance, but be about the place in role. We realised that in this way codes of behaviour, attitudes, manners and etiquette could swiftly be conveyed to the children who took part. It is one thing to be told on a guided

tour of an old building of the difference between the heat and noise of a busy kitchen and the tranquility of the apartments reserved for the owner. It is quite another way of learning to prepare a hot drink on an open fire in the kitchen and carry it through the corridors to the inner area, meeting on your way the housekeeper who inspects and approves the brew and finally the person for whom it was intended, who receives it politely but imperiously.

At Heveningham Hall, to the organisation of which we will return, we intended to open up the widest possible view of a society at work. We were also committed to the idea of setting up the reconstruction from local resources. The whole project was to be a piece of community education, meeting the needs of 9-13 year olds, but involving younger and older pupils, and their teachers, people from the local community, students from the nearby University of East Anglia. We were against the notion of specialists, *Living History Experts,* and much more interested in discovering a model, a way of research and learning which could be used by other teachers in other contexts. We accepted the limitations of the building, and whatever equipment and objects were available. The inspiration was to believe that it could be done, and that those who took part would learn from it.

Orford Castle dominates a sand and shingle estuary on the Suffolk coast. It was completed in 1176 by Henry II as a testament to his strength and

power in this corner of East Anglia. What remains of the castle now is the keep, an imposing octagonal stone tower rising through three floors. From the roof of the tower, the land falls in a series of steep folds, indicating the presence of walls and fortification. The castle is much visited by school parties who explore the empty rooms, move up and down the stone staircases investigating the details and features which remain or have been restored. How much do these visits reveal to the children of life as it might have been in the twelfth and thirteenth centuries? Encouraged by the success of the Heveningham project we were asked by local teachers to devise a scheme to set up a reconstruction at Orford. The difference was that at Heveningham the building was intact, but at Orford little remained. It was not credible to inhabit the single tower as if it were a complete castle. Besides, the monument had to remain open to the public during the day.

The solution was this decision. So little of the castle remains, not because it has fallen down, but the year is 1173, and it has not yet been fully built. What followed from that idea was the need for a twelfth century encampment of builders in the grounds of the castle. About 400 metres from the keep was a small clearing wedged between lines of high trees. This was where the work on the fortification would begin. It was the summer of 1173, fortification and protection of the site were more important than extending the keep, that work could wait until the winter. Groups of children would come to the encampment for the day to work as apprentices. Here they would undertake stone work, build a wooden gate tower, make clay pots, fashion weapons with the armourer, cook on open fires the food of the period. In role would be the Constable and his Deputy, receiving supplies from the tenant of a nearby imaginary manor house. Providing the supplies would be witness of her loyalty to the King— Henry II. Sending short measure could suggest treachery. Again the emphasis would be upon learning by doing, this process extended by using the elementary role play of a drama lesson to investigate the attitudes and behaviour of the twelfth century society. Here we were using part of a monument, choosing to use the castle as a setting and background for the reconstruction, rather than, as at Heveningham, using the building itself. In both cases, we sought a simple pattern of organisation to enable us to meet our aims.

ORGANISING THE DAY

Publicity

The information which went to the schools was as follows:

Heveningham Hall
Midsummer 1790
A Suffolk Schools Project.

eveningham Hall – a large 18th century house designed by James Wyatt and Robert Taylor with grounds by Capability Brown will, between June 30th and July 4th this summer, be the centre of a project for schools in Suffolk. The Hall, gardens and grounds will be used for a detailed reconstruction of life in a rural community at the end of the eighteenth century, and the intention is to give children from local schools a vivid insight into life and work at the Hall as it would have been in the summer of 1790. History, drama, art, music and environmental studies will combine in a single project and Heveningham opened for a week to parties of children in the middle school age range (9-13). Groups will be able to spend the whole of one day at the Hall, taking part in a range of activities and events which will be led by a team of teachers, actors and musicians. The project is being organised by the Drama Advisory Services based at Lowestoft.

ll the children who take part will be involved as participants rather than as spectators, and we shall be imagining that they have been recruited as servants for the day by the owners of Heveningham in 1790. On arrival at the Hall, the visitors will be met in the courtyard by the owner, his family and household staff, who will be dressed in clothes of the 18th century. From there, the children will divide into groups of ten, collect a simple costume, and move off into the house and grounds to begin the day's work. Each small group will be led and supervised by a teacher from the project, and as far as possible work will be with the tools and equipment which would have been available in 1790.

he visitors are likely to find themselves working with cooks in the kitchen to prepare food, sorting out rooms with the house servants or perhaps helping a carpenter to build and repair furniture. Outside, others will be with gamekeepers stocking and clearing the lake, or with gardeners amongst the trees, shrubs and vegetables in the walled garden. Maintenance of the stables, orangery and ice-house will have to be undertaken, trees will need measuring, examining and replacing.

fter lunch, each group will turn to a second activity, so that all will have an opportunity to work both indoors and out in the grounds. At the end of the day, everyone will gather to watch a short performance devised and presented by a group of actors and musicians. Their performance will recapture something of the style, pre-occupations and perils of life in 18th century England.

hroughout the day the participants will brush up against other characters who might have lived around, or been visiting the Hall. Peddlars poachers and entertainers are likely to be seen, as are guardians of law and order and people from the neighbouring village. Some of them will arrive in horse-drawn carriage. The day's programme will begin at 9.30 and end around 2.30 in time for a return to individual schools near the end of the school day.

efore the visit to the Hall, each child will get a copy of "The Huntingfield Times" a newspaper prepared in the style of an eighteenth century journal, which is designed as a source of background information about life in England two hundred years ago. Where possible, one of the teachers from the project will visit the schools attending, in the costume and character of an eighteenth century tradesman, to talk to and work with the children.

n essential part of the project is the involvement of the children as participants, and so that this can be as thorough and effective as possible, only two hundred places are available each day. A charge of £1.20 per head is being made for the visit, part of this goes to the National Trust, the remainder to cover the cost of setting up the week. Individual schools should make their own arrangements for bringing groups to the Hall.

taff from the county's peripatetic teaching team will be working with the children and they will be joined by the Theatre in Education team from The Wolsey Theatre, Ipswich, a group from Lowestoft Theatre Centre, members of staff and pupils from local High Schools, as well as a number of local musicians, craftsmen and helpers. The team is grateful to Charles Sheppard the Administrator at Heveningham Hall for his help and advice, and to the Department of the Environment and National Trust for allowing the building to be used. Project Team: Patrick Redsell June Bowry, Advisory Service. John Fairclough, Museum Service, Rory Kelsey, Paul Hobbs, Frances Nerini, Michael Richardson, Lowestoft Theatre Centre.

he local village - Huntingfield is organising a Country Faire on Saturday July 5th at the end of the week. The Faire will be attended by many of the characters in costume from the project, and will have the settings and style of the late 18th century. We hope that this event which will last from noon until dusk, will give parents and visitors an opportunity to share the amosphere of the week. Details of the Faire are contained in the Huntingfield Times.

The Working Groups

It was an early decision that not all the participants would experience all the activities. It seemed better to do two activities thoroughly than to scratch at six or seven. Each school was asked to send a list of the children who would be taking part. We then divided the children around the twenty working groups, making no distinction between work undertaken by boys or girls. (This is historically inaccurate, but the project is taking place *now,* and encompasses today's needs as well as those of the past). Children from one school would experience the day in different ways. If you were working by the lake, you might see a carriage arrive in the distance at the front of the house. If you were a house servant you might meet and unload the carriage, but miss the pike being caught in the lake. There is purpose in this. We wanted the children to exchange information, to *build up* their experience by talking with each other after the visit. This development process is expanded in the section "After the Visit - Evaluation and Development."

TASKS OF WORKING GROUPS

Heveningham Hall
Midsummer 1790
A Suffolk Schools Project.

The Indoor Groups

Name	Tasks
Butler	Errands, messages, service of meals, collection of ice from the ice house, meeting and attending visitors, co-ordinating household activities.
Housekeeper	Cleaning and preparing house, opening and preparing visitors' rooms, silver and glass ware, accounts, deliveries, ordering supplies. Care of the sick household members.
Kitchen I (Hot)	Preparation of simple meals over a range—Breakfast—toast and drinks, Luncheon—rabbit skinning and vegetables, hot water for family needs.
Kitchen II (Cold)	Preparation of cold foods, butter, cheese, desserts, cold drinks, preserving, cold buffet.
Launderer/Weaver	Collection of dirty linen, washing, drying and ironing (charcoal iron), using traditional methods. Loom weaving.
Maria-Vanneck's Maid	Waking, washing, dressing Lady Vanneck. Preparing and fetching meals, cleaning inner apartments and domestic duties using traditional methods.
Surveyor	Surveying for landscaping, building survey and repair using traditional techniques, designing outdoor and indoor improvements.
Plasterer	Making mouldings, interior decoration, traditional plaster work.
Footman/Seamstress	Tailoring and clothing repair, maintenance of furniture, cleaning floor coverings, care of indoor fires, unpacking visitors' baggage.
Nursery	Care and education of Vanneck children (local primary school children in role). Toys, games, food and medicines for owners' children.

The Outdoor Groups

Name	Tasks
Carpenter	Construction of sedan chair, building wooden wheelbarrow, tool sharpening (grindstone), repair of garden tools, barrels, etc. (link with Butler)
Osierworker	Making besoms, rush lights, fencing, baskets, eel traps, kitchen and household cleaning equipment (link with Housekeeper and Lakeman).
Blacksmith	Care of horses and carriages, care of yard animals, chickens, dogs, goats (link with Gamekeeper/Constable).
Gardener 1	Care of lawns, flower beds, measuring, digging, tending, using traditional implements and wisdom (link with Housekeeper).
Gardener 2	Growing, tending, collecting and preparation of vegetables and herbs for kitchens and Herbalist/Dyer.
Herbalist/Dyer	Spinning and dyeing wools sent by shepherd, using vegetables and plants from estate. Preparation of herbal medicines, ointments, cures, and remedies (link with Nursery).
Charcoal Burner	Making charcoal for kitchens and other fire users. Constructing charcoal mounds. (link with Kitchens).
Shepherd	Care, driving and penning of sheep. Clipping with hand clippers, care of wool. (link with Dyer and Weaver).
Lakeman	Cutting reeds for thatch and rush lights, fishing, boat repairs, eel trapping. Care of woodland, follyes, provision of timber for charcoal burner, construction of *Follye Faire*.
Brewman	Brewing, bottling, cider making, cordial making.

Each working group would be led by one adult in role. In some cases this was a local teacher attached to the project, in others, it was someone from the community with particular skills who agreed to take part. Often local high school pupils from the 4th and 5th year worked in a particular group for a week. The work of each group centred around tasks to accomplish within an hour and a half. It was important that all children found something to do as soon as they joined their group.

For this reason, we have found that the ratio of one to ten is a successful one. At Heveningham there were 20 working groups—200 children but you could equally well have just two working groups, 20 children and 2 adults working in one space. Thus the day was divided into working halves, preceded by an introduction, the assembly in the courtyard, which set the atmosphere and expectations of the day.

The Group Leaders

We were fortunate to be allowed a small number of teachers who were attached for a week to the project. They became group leaders, often researching and developing a hobby so that it could be an activity. The Brewman (from a middle school) was an enthusiastic home brewer and winemaker who was able to research quickly and easily and then experiment with traditional materials and techniques. Another teacher from a middle school had always wanted to experiment with charcoal making. He had taught the principle from books for some time, now he was able to experiment. A primary teacher had a forge at home. He adapted some straightforward techniques and brought them to the project. He was also the only person who could easily and successfully milk the goat! The Lakeman was the head of a primary school with an enthusiasm and talent for local environmental studies. He and the children in his group were experimenting with eighteenth century fishing techniques. They were astonished to find a golden carp on the end of one of the lines on the second day. But not all the leaders were teachers. Any community has many members who have a traditional skill as an interest. It did not prove difficult to find weavers, spinners, gardeners, seamstresses. Often they were prepared to lend their own specialist equipment. Where they felt unsure about supervising a group of ten children, we divided the group between two

complimentary tasks. Hence the Herbalist worked with the Dyer, the Launderer with the Weaver. It is important to divide groups, tasks and time into units with which leaders can feel comfortable. A key factor in this process was the decision to divide the day into two halves, so that an individual group leader could work with one group of ten children for 1½ hours before breaking for lunch, and then in the afternoon repeat, continue or extend the work with another group of ten. The next day the process began again. Each group was linked with an outdoor or indoor unit and exchanged with them. This made the organisation easier. The children and their group leaders knew from the outset where they would go after lunch. It is essential to build these secure points into the organisation of the day.

A further support was the attachment of a few high school pupils (often 4th or 5th year students) to various working groups. Sometimes this was a condition of being allowed a teacher from a school for a week. She or he would come with a class. It was fascinating process to watch the 15 or 16 year olds who may consider themselves above taking part in an event like this, taking responsibility for one or two younger children, helping with the more difficult and dangerous tasks. Our guess is

that the research, discovery and learning is as important for this group as it is for younger children.

The Actors' Role

There is one key factor in the contribution of the actors. They are in role, in the background, and must not give a performance nor intimidate the children who are taking part. In the following summary of their day, it is clear how low key the events of the day have to be. They must set in context the work of the groups but not overwhelm it. Providing a firm framework for the day and a reason for the various activities is their purpose.

When Lady Jane Vanneck is stung by a bee in the courtyard, it is the most dramatic event of the day, needing the attention of the Housekeeper and her staff, as well as the help of the Herbalist, but equally setting in place the work of the Gardeners who have been tending and gathering medicinal herbs.

The wagers between Sir Joshua Vanneck and the visitor Captain Wright over whose servants are most fleet of foot, draws the assembly of the Butler's staff and the Footmen, but the Gardeners may not stop working to watch. They will probably see sovereigns change hands between Sir Joshua and Captain Wright, and reflect on the

pauper who was found asleep in one of the garden sheds earlier in the day.

The Plot of the Day—The Actor's Briefing

We selected a specific date in the past as the occasion for the reconstruction and used as many actual known facts as we could as the basis for the story. We had to fill out that evidence in order to provide a programme of events for the day, but we did not alter or distort the facts so far as we can ascertain them from historical texts and sources available in the record offices and museums. This involved much research during the preparation of the project both into specific local events and into the background of the period. This is itself given wider application in the provision of resource material for teachers to use in schools before and after the day of the project.

The leading characters were Sir Joshua and Lady Maria Vanneck who lived at Heveningham with their two daughters of *marriageable age* . . . Jane and Elizabeth. Elizabeth, the younger, has an interest in the sufferings of the poor. Her independence of mind is a source of concern to her parents. Jane is quiet, demure, polite, content to be part of the society in which she lives.

Heveningham is visited by Captain Wright, who lives for the greater part of the year in London, and is visiting the house at Sir Joshua's request. He has heard of the two daughters, is taken with the growing fashion for things of the country, and wishes to see for himself what inspiration he may draw from a few days at Heveningham. Another visitor expected at the Hall is Thomas Vine, an assistant of Capability Brown, who is to have discussions with Sir Joshua about improvements to the lake and grounds. In the nursery, the younger children are at play with their nurse, well removed from the pauper who is about in the grounds.

The family and their visitors take lunch.

Heveningham Hall
Midsummer 1790
A Suffolk Schools Project.

The timetable for the actors had to be planned in detail :-

10.00	Group Leaders in Courtyard. Maria asleep. Sir Joshua, Housekeeper, Elizabeth and Jane to courtyard.
10.10	Servants tour house.
10.15	Sir Joshua, Elizabeth and Jane wander to lawns. Lady Maria is awoken.
10.30	Sir Joshua, Elizabeth and Jane inspect servants in study. Breakfast is ordered. Pauper discovered in garden shed.
10.40	Breakfast served to Sir Joshua, Elizabeth and Jane in study. Mr. Vine arrives in courtyard, met by Butler's servants, carriage unloaded.
10.50	Sir Joshua meets Mr. Vine in salon, looks at charts. Elizabeth to gardens to encounter pauper. Jane to gardens to sketch.
11.00	Mr. Vine to lake to inspect possibilities of improvement. Captain Wright arrives at main entrance. Elizabeth arrives at main entrance with pauper.
11.05	Captain Wright to rooms to supervise unpacking. Elizabeth to Lady Maria's rooms to be reprimanded. Sir Joshua to study to reprimand Butler. Pauper to courtyard. Puppeteer to lawns to entertain young children.
11.10	Sir Joshua wanders. Jane returns from gardens. Elizabeth wanders in courtyard area.
11.20	Sir Joshua, Lady Maria, Elizabeth and Jane meet Captain Wright in library for refreshments.
11.30	LUNCH
12.00	Elizabeth and Jane meet Mr. Vine in gardens for landscape design lesson.

12.15	Sir Joshua and Jane take carriage to lake and then to Follye, meeting Mr. Vine en route. Pauper to lake area. Elizabeth takes singing lesson in salon. Lady Maria strolls and talks with Captain Wright on lawns.
12.35	Lady Maria to rooms to rest and be attended.
12.40	Jane to courtyard, receives bee sting, is taken to house. Elizabeth wanders in house. Sir Joshua and Captain Wright stroll and talk on lawns. Mr. Vine encounters pauper.
12.45	Captain Wright, Sir Joshua to gardens. Wager on running footmen.
12.50	Running Race in gardens.
1.00	Elizabeth and Captain Wright stroll and talk in gardens and on lawns. Sir Joshua meets Lady Maria in library. Jane rests in open air. Pauper to kitchen area. Mr. Vine to gardens to reprimand gardener.
1.10	Sir Joshua and Lady Maria to lawns, take refreshment. Captain Wright and Elizabeth enter house. Captain Wright to rooms to pack and prepare for departure. Elizabeth and Jane to salon to discuss Captain Wright.
1.25	Captain Wright departs.
1.30	Vanneck family to study.
1.45	Family entertains the servants.

What the Children did

We chose a week early in July as being most likely to give us good weather! Over a number of years we have discovered that the weather in late June and early July is more often dry than wet, and that when it does rain it seldom rains all day.

Heveningham Hall has survived with remarkably little alteration for almost 200 years. The exterior was completed in 1780 to designs by Sir Robert Taylor, and the interior was designed by James Wyatt with painting by Biaggio Rebecca. The grounds were landscaped in 1781 by Capability Brown, who also designed the stable yard and the ice house. Wyatt built an elegant orangery. As there have been no major alterations since the work of these masters, Heveningham survives as one of the finest examples in England of the skills and imagination that went into eighteenth century buildings.

Each morning for the week of the project we checked that all evidence of the nineteenth and twentieth centuries was concealed. Sacking hid the National Trust's sign guiding visitors to the tea rooms or the gardens, and was carefully draped over the petrol pump. The old kitchen was transformed from National Trust shop to eighteenth century dairy (a process that had to be reversed every afternoon when the Hall opened to the public at 2.00 p.m.). Fires were lit in several grates. By 9.15 all staff cars had been removed from their garages in the stable yard and one or more horse-drawn vehicles had arrived.

At 9.30 the day's complement of 200 children, in the age range 9-13, started to arrive. In Capability Brown's stable yard they found straw on the cobbles, a carpenter's shop ready for work, a sedan chair partly built, and a group of senior servants (actors and teachers in eighteenth-century costume). Girls collected aprons and bonnets, boys donned waistcoats and they formed groups of ten or so attached to each servant. From now on they were living in the eighteenth century as servants at the Hall. As soon as all the children had arrived the owner of the Hall, Sir Joshua Vanneck, and his family entered the yard and greeted the assembled servants. Then it was the turn of the housekeeper to remind them to carry out their orders promptly, to bow or curtsy when they met members of the family (they all had to practise this), and with a final warning to 'let there be no cause for complaint', she left the butler to lead all the groups on a brief tour through the main rooms. This gave them all an idea of the layout of the Hall and a chance to see all the State Rooms because from now on they would go only into rooms to which their tasks took them.

Half the groups worked inside the house. Their duties included waking and dressing the lady of the house, preparing and serving food for the family, cleaning rooms, attending to the fires, running errands—in fact meeting all the needs of an eighteenth century family, who could be very demanding and with whom there could be no arguing. If his lordship reprimanded the butler, his group soon found themselves in trouble and so

did those of his juniors. The children not only saw the hierarchy of the household, they became part of it.

We had to work within the limitations of what was available, both in the way of space and equipment. Hence, an empty room on the second floor in which plasterwork and decoration were in very poor condition became home for the plasterer, who set up a couple of trestle tables, hung some dust sheets across the windows, lit candles and worked with the children on techniques of plaster moulding. Before they could begin, however, they had to fetch jugs and buckets of water from the well in the courtyard. An old housekeeper's room, with its cooking range intact, became the *hot* kitchen, full of pans, steaming water, hot chocolate simmering on the hob. The group leader (an Advisory Teacher for early years) lined the cupboards with copies of the Huntingfield Times and put together a cookbook. The actual house kitchen from which the range had been removed became the *cold kitchen,* a place for butter and cheese making.

Meanwhile the other groups were working in the grounds and gardens. On hot days they found how much heat the high brick walls kept in the walled garden where they hoed and planted. Herbs were gathered, honey and beeswax were prepared, paths were swept, sheep were tended, fish were caught in the lake.

In the courtyard, every available shed or old stable was transformed into a place of work or shelter, modern garden machinery was hidden behind old barrels, bales of straw, or covered with calico and hessian. Both inside the house and out in the gardens, where an area was too delicate or fragile to be used, we closed it, where necessary hinted that it was under repair or re-decoration and worked elsewhere. The arts of substitution and compromise were deployed to their fullest extent. The important thing is to use what is available, keep it busy and exclude the rest. Where light fittings, radiators, heaters or modern conversions intrude too fiercely, do not attempt to disguise them, avoid using the space.

Nowhere was life completely undisturbed. When his lordship demanded a cold drink, the butler wasted no time in sending a message to the kitchens, but then the carpenter, along with his group, had to be distracted from making a deadfall mouse-trap or working on the sedan chair because it was his task to fetch ice from the ice house. During a hot week the supply of ice (diverted from Lowestoft fish stores, instead of being gathered from the lake during a suitable winter) survived perfectly in Capability Brown's magnificent thatched ice house.

Just as garden staff were starting work the local constable arrived to warn them against poaching and demonstrated the perils of the mantrap. When the head gardener practically lost his voice, the herbalist and her group presented him with a special preparation of honey and herbs which he had to consume in their presence—it was actually very effective! A vagrant appeared several times

and was finally seized and flogged for stealing from the kitchen. Every morning his lordship's eldest son arrived in his carriage, complete with his luggage which had to be unpacked for him. In the afternoon his departure created additional work for the household.

At 11.30 the children returned to the twentieth century for long enough to eat their sandwiches, before the morning's indoor groups started work outdoors and the outdoor groups formed the indoor staff for the afternoon. The lunchbreak was enlivened by an eighteenth century Punch and Judy show and other period entertainments.

In the afternoon the children worked as servants until 2.00, when they all assembled on a sloping lawn behind the Hall. For the first time during a busy day they became simply spectators. They watched a short play about eighteenth century life performed by the eighteenth century Vanneck family. After this, they returned to their schools and the Hall returned to the twentieth century.

At Orford, where there were no working spaces, a simple shelter using five poles, rope guys and a large piece of white canvas was constructed by the site crew (from a local high school) for each group.

The Midday Meal

One problem that emerged during the Heveningham project was the total break at midday caused by stopping for lunch. Children abandoned their eighteenth century roles and left the working areas to consume the sandwiches they had brought for their packed lunches. Although we attempted to retain some of the period atmosphere by staging appropriate entertainments such as Punch and Judy, it took a determined effort to recapture the correct feel in the afternoon. Afterwards, one of the authors was involved in a Tudor project *Wolsey at Ipswich 1529* during which the atmosphere was preserved by having a set lunch provided by the school meals service which the children had to eat under the strict discipline of a Tudor schoolmaster. This seemed to work, so it was a logical extension to make the midday meal an integral part of the Bigod project. In this case an important morning task for the two kitchen groups was to prepare a simple medieval meal for the entire encampment. They boiled large quantities of medieval soup, using vegetables and herbs that would have been available locally, cut up carrots, cheese and apples. Bulk quantities of ingredients were ordered through the school meals service and other items were purchased from local grocers. A local baker produced fresh trencher bread every day to an agreed recipe, because although we had a group baking on the site it was impossible for them to produce the amount required for everybody, so they concentrated on small delicacies.

At the appropriate time the chaplain said grace, in Latin of course, and used his role to give instructions about collecting the food and about the disposal of any waste in the correct rubbish pits. The working groups were called up individually to join the queues at the kitchen, and then went back to eat in their working areas. Only then was a short break created because the pupils' own teachers were asked to take them back to the toilets in the nearby primary school. This solved an essential problem and gave the group leaders a break from working with the children! As the break was brief and devoted to one practical purpose it did not really spoil the continuity of the working day. The children quickly settled into their afternoon task back in the medieval atmosphere. It is clearly important to build into any project which lasts longer than half a day provision for the midday meal, for access to toilets and for the groups leaders to have a break.

Equipment

As far as possible the equipment and furnishings used in the projects are the real things. Just as there is value in using the actual location with the correct historical associations, so it is a great help to use the original objects that were used at the time. This is acceptable when the originals are not too valuable or too fragile, but if they are not available then modern copies have been purchased to provide items that are as near as possible in design and materials to the originals. Original items and prototypes for copies mostly came from the collections of Suffolk Museum Education Service, Ipswich Museums and the Museum of East Anglian Life at Stowmarket.

For the Heveningham project it was possible to use a large number of original objects and the majority of the reproductions could be purchased from suppliers of crockery and kitchen equipment who specialise in *Seconds*. For the Bigod project there was little original medieval equipment available, although contemporary drawings show that the designs of many traditional craft tools have changed little, and nineteenth century examples were similar to those of the twelfth century. However much of the pottery and furniture had to be made especially for us. Fortunately we found a local potter prepared to fulfil such orders as *150 medieval soup bowls*. The research, design and manufacture of *reproductive* objects could be a high school project. The main consideration with reproduction items is to ensure that they are made from the right materials and to appropriate designs. The fact that they may be raw and unworn does not matter as we sometimes forget that all these things were new and in good condition when they were first made.

The water supply is an important consideration in this type of project. At Heveningham we were able to revive the old hand cranked pump to draw water from the well, although for modern purposes it had been superseded by an electric pump. The need to crank the pump reminded modern youngsters that an automatic water supply has not always been available. At Orford it was not possible to use the orginal well in the keep, although in theory this was the source of the fresh water stored in large barrels in the encampment. In fact these barrels, as well as the open half barrels which were used for everything except drinking and cooking, were filled with fresh water every evening by the local fire brigade. A number of small barrels were used to carry water round the site and to bring fresh supplies from the primary school. Whenever possible these were transported by horse and cart which added to the authenticity of the scene. The need to conserve water because of the problems in supplying it was continually stressed during the project. A number of strong wooden buckets to carry water and wet materials around the site were essential to the operation of the scheme. In fact for all historical reconstructions the organisers need to ensure that they have an adequate water supply and authentic barrels and buckets for storing and transporting liquid. (See Page 27 for suppliers). A very important consideration in equipping such projects has to be the elimination of modern materials. It is surprisingly difficult to ensure that no plastic bowls or cardboard boxes are used in the working areas. Plenty of suitable alternatives such as wooden boxes and earthenware bowls have to be available. It is also necessary to check that tools have wooden, not plastic, handles.

Administration of the Day

The practical organisation of the day requires very careful planning based on a detailed timetable, but with provision for flexibility when delays occur. First of all it is essential to plan starting and finishing times in consultation with the teachers, as transport arrangements will limit the possibilities. Once times are fixed it must be emphasised to teachers that when several schools are involved on the same day they should make every effort to arrive promptly or the others will be kept waiting, and that nobody can leave this sort of project before the end. We generally find it possible to fix the arrival time for the children at about 9.30 a.m. and to finish by 3.00 p.m., but some allowance has to be made for coach companies that fail to allow sufficient time for the journey or insist on trying to book their vehicles for two trips at the same time.

Once the pupils arrive the first task is to get them into costume. At Orford we were fortunate that the local primary school is only separated from the castle by a playingfield. Children got into their costumes in the school playground, or on wet days in the hall—by courtesy of a very helpful headmaster. They were helped by some of the group leaders, and were then told to find correct working groups for the morning session. The groups were identified by large banners displayed in the playground, and lists showing the division into groups had been sent to schools well in advance. However it is essential to have a master list in the oganiser's hand as it can be the last school to arrive that has not told the children which group they are to join or has muddled the instructions. This can be a difficult moment for the organiser because if group leaders have been told to expect to work with ten children they can reasonably complain when twenty crowd round them, and the organiser has to use the list to sort things out. Occasionally he needs to assure an uncertain child, with a confidence that he may not really feel, that the child's costume does fit and that he is in the right group.

Once the children are in costume and in their groups the day can start. From this moment onwards all the adults must behave in their correct period role as the children will quickly take a lead from them. A quick check on the time—a large sleeve can conceal the vital but anachronistic watch—will show whether the morning's event can run to the original timetable. If corrections to the timing are needed now or later, to allow for unexpected contingencies, the organisers have to give discreet warnings to the actors and the group leaders. On the Bigod project it was found to be helpful to have the chaplain, as part of his role, ring his bell and call out the time at certain intervals while encouraging the apprentices to work at their tasks. Group leaders knew the significance of any variations in his message and, as his office gave him direct access to the Constable and the other principal characters, he could arrange any adjustments in their timings.

Any arrivals from outside the project area have to be carefully timed so that the *unexpected visiting knight* or the cartload of provisions arrive when required. The successful operation of the day depends upon the strict framework of the timetable being tempered by reasonable flexibility of the main characters within their roles to allow for occasional unpredictable delays.

Heveningham Hall
Midsummer 1790
A Suffolk Schools Project.

Equipment for Working Groups

Indoors

Name	Equipment
Butler	Cutlery, Candlesticks, Candle Snuffers Brass Trays, Books (leather-bound), Inkstand, Tinder Box, Bucket.
Housekeeper	Tea Urn, Tea Caddy, Wash Stand, Trivets, Cleaning Materials.
Kitchen I (Hot)	Kettles, Saucepans, Boiling Pots, Ladles, Strainer, Chopping Boards, Pestles and Mortars, Sugar Cutters, Roasting Jack, Jugs, Bowls, Plates, Wooden Spoons, Storage Jars, Buckets.
Kitchen II (Cold)	Butter Churns, Butter Mould, Butter Hands, Butter Stamps, Milk Pans, Cream Fleeters, Jugs, Bowls, Scales, Butter Muslin, Storage Jars, Buckets, Whisks.
Launderer	Wash Tubs, Charcoal Irons, Box Irons, Flat Irons, Pans of Charcoal, Buckets, Clothes Pegs, Baskets.
Surveyor	Drawing Board, Rulers, Set Square, Planetable, Gunter's Chain.
Footman	Feather Dusters, Brooms, Polishing Set, Tinder Box, Leather Boots and Polish, Trays, Brushes, Buckets.
Nursery	Toys, Model Theatre, Slates and Slate Pencils, Balls, Hoops.

Outdoors

Name	Equipment
Carpenter	Woodworking Planes, Hammers, Grindstone, Deadfall Mousetrap, Parts for Sedan Chair, Pole Lathe, Glue Pot, Gouges.
Osierworker	Choppers, Axes, Strong Knives.
Gardener	Hoes, Rakes, Dibblers, Gunter's Chain, Bird-scaring Rattles, Traps, Weeding Hooks, Besoms, Baskets, Buckets.
Shepherd	Spring Shears, Root Chopper, Hurdles.
Herbalist/Dyer	Boiling Pots, Materials and Herbs for Dyes and Potions, Bowls, Chopping Boards, Knives, Pestles and Mortars, Baskets.
Charcoal Burner	Saw, Wedges, Hammer, Spade.
Lakeman	Eel Pritches, Fishing Hooks and Lines, Traps made from Osiers, Weed Drag, Rake, Axe, Choppers.
Brewman	Jugs, Bowls, Jars, Chopping Boards, Knives, Barrels, Buckets, Funnels, Bottles, Boiling Pots.

PREPARING FOR THE VISIT

Earlier, we have written of how important it is to see the day of the visit and participation as part of a much longer period of research into the period under scrutiny. We do not believe that a day spent at a *living history* project replaces the more familiar skills of research—using resource books, writing and compilation, discussion, classroom drama and art work. We do however believe that many of these ways of working are enriched and made more enjoyable to more pupils because they are part of a longer, deeper and more accessible approach. It is worth noting how demanding the skills of evidence collection, interpretation or even writing can be for many pupils; who find they cannot make sense of the data quickly and lose interest. If on the other hand you have spent a day working at Heveningham or Orford Castle, returning to the resource books to compare what you have seen and done with eighteenth or twelfth century evidence is a fascinating experience. This *build up* process is an important characteristic of the projects. (The follow-up work is covered in the next section.)

Finding appropriate source material, illustrations, writing, maps, objects, for children and gathering it together in one place for any length of time is a time consuming process. Teachers have a demanding and busy pattern of work and seldom have long periods of time to gather everything they would like the children to see and hear before the day's visit. We saw the need for a straightforward, interesting and accessible booklet to provide the eighteenth century background. We needed a publication which would seize something of the style of language, give accounts of the society and above all, something which was cheap to produce. The format which met most of these needs for the Heveningham project was that of a newspaper. So the *Huntingfield Times* was born. A team of local teachers searched old copies of the Ipswich Gazette for articles which could be re-written in a concise and lucid style. Incidents and description from eighteenth century novels became the inspiration for short written pieces or advertisements. Museum objects were drawn by a local graphic artist and appeared as newspaper illustrations (wrong for the period, but right for the project). See Page 28.

Meeting the Huntingfield Village Committee gave rise to another idea. On the Saturday following the project week, the village would hold a *Country Faire* on the field facing Heveningham Hall. Children and characters in costume and role would attend, demonstrate and perhaps sell things made from Monday to Friday. Sir Joshua Vanneck and his family would open the Faire. The preparation of this Faire would be a small part of the work of the week. Sir Joshua was constructing a small *follye,* opposite the hall and would declare it completed at 2.00 p.m. on Saturday. In this way, many members of the local community became involved in *Midsummer 1790.* The Faire was advertised in the Huntingfield Times and offers of help with the loan of horses, equipment and materials followed. It is significant how much more detailed the project became as a result of this early involvement of people outside the education service.

When teachers booked places (in March/April), for a day at the project they also committed themselves to attending a number of in-service sessions at a local Teachers' Centre early in the summer term. One of those meetings was devoted to details of the organisation, but the other two were used to prepare the background. A copy of the Huntingfield Times was available for each child who would take part. Together, the teachers looked at ways of using the newspaper for individual and group work. Clothes and costumes were discussed. Many of the schools agreed to make up half a dozen costumes from bolts of fabric which had been purchased. They took back to school simple illustrated patterns, (see illustration on page 34), agreed to allow the costumes they made to be pooled and used by each day's participants. The making of these clothes became part of the research process for many children, as did searching through the Huntingfield Times to find stories or information about the trade you would take up for the day at the Hall. By this time the children knew which working groups they would join. In some schools classroom drama and simple role play was used by teachers to bring to life small incidents from the newspaper so that feelings and attitudes could be explored.

We still felt however the need for a bridge between these activities and the *experience* of the day. A number of local amateur actors helped. In the role and clothes of a particular trade—carpenter, launderer, housekeeper, they visited each class for an hour or so to talk about life and work at Heveningham. The carpenter carried his bag of tools, the housekeeper her accounts and some cleaning materials. The children asked many questions and gradually the idea of being in the role for the day was conveyed to them. These visitors in role were able to introduce a style of language to the young visitors which indicated that English *now* is not entirely what it was *then.* They had already glimpsed this from the newspaper but now they were confronted with it, and so introduced to ideas about codes of behaviour being transmitted by language. Our 1790 language was diluted from the original and we did not expect the children on the day of their visit to mimic it, but we hoped that the group leaders would use it, and that it would be one more point of discussion and comparison for the children after their visit.

At Orford Castle, we decided that the children would attend as apprentices. This pressed the case for an alternative approach to that of the newspaper.

Two publications emerged—An Apprentices Manual (Page 32) which gave an anatomy of the Castle and its operation, as well as details of the work and duties required of the apprentices. This was supported by a Teachers Handbook and the two were supplemented by a simple snakes and ladders type board game which could be played wih dice and counters by groups of up to six children. Landing a group of soldiers at Dunwich (represented by your counter) you had to advance them across a map of Suffolk to Bungay, falling back if you landed on a hazard square, advancing if you found yourself on a luck square. *Retreat* and *Advance* cards gave authentic reasons for hasty or impeded progress. Each visitor received a copy of the Apprentices Manual. Boardgames and Handbooks were retained around the participating schools. In each case, the cost of printing was absorbed into the admission price.

The preparation and production of these background materials as well as of equipment could well be an enjoyable task for pupils from a neighbourhood High School, College of Further Education, or one of the Adult Centres in the area. Schools were supplied with illustrated instructions for making twelfth century clothes for the children (see Page 35).

We remain convinced that the more people from the many organisations in the community that are involved, the greater the value of the project as community education. Asking for the involvement of others involves explaining the educational principles which underly the project. Achieving their constructive involvement in the preparation and organisation of the event shares, informs, explains. From this flows understanding and goodwill.

AFTER THE VISIT — EVALUATION AND DEVELOPMENT

Evaluation of the major projects is important. At its most obvious it is notable that teachers who have been once are eager to bring classes in future years. After the project, children discussed among themselves at great length what they had experienced and done during the day in a way that contributed to their language skills as well as their understanding of history. Teachers have said that the children were anxious to talk about and share their experiences for many days afterwards. This was deliberately encouraged in the organisation of the work areas by distributing pupils from each school among the various groups so that they did not all see all the same events and they had different experiences to compare. They could talk about how these fitted together to create a total picture of what happened during the days. This oral work is of key importance.

When it has been possible to visit schools afterwards it has been clear that a variety of oral, written and craft work has been undertaken as a direct result of the project, and much of it has been of a high standard. After the *Wolsey at Ipswich,* project, one of the authors visited all fifteen schools that participated, and discussion with the children showed enormous retention of the experience combined with enthusiasm and understanding. Clearly most of the children who took part learnt from the experience and found it a thoroughly enjoyable day helping to bring a historical monument to life in a very real way.

In general, children learn best when they discover something for themselves through their own experience. The reconstruction of the past is one way to widen children's experience and to enable them to participate in some aspects of life in a previous century.

It is this attempt to guide the children to an imaginative grasp of the past, and to a more penetrating understanding of life as it *was,* compared to what it *is,* which characterises the use of reconstruction.

In this method of learning there are three distinct, but interrelated, stages which the children must complete :-

    A. Preparation and research.
    B. Participation in the Project.
    C. Evaluation of the experience and extension from it.

Increasingly in schools we are seeking to move the study of history away from learning strings of dates and facts, towards understanding certain key concepts and acquiring useful skills. One of these skills is the use of evidence, but in history we never have all the evidence on which to decide exactly what happened and why it happened as it did, and much of the evidence is not concrete. Pupils need to develop a disciplined historical imagination to bring together the available evidence in such a way that they can understand the attitudes and feelings of people other than themselves in situations very different from their own.

If we can do this, then we can give them the feel of life in a particular period, so that they know what it was like to be alive then.

In this process drama and role play are paramount. They are rational and disciplined methods of research. By taking on elementary roles, by stepping into the shoes of other people, you have to deal with the problems of that time with the resources of that time. If the context is accurate, you meet and experience something of the feelings which preoccupied people in the past. With skillful guidance it is possible to lead children to create an imagined world which they can inhabit and learn from. The learning and development is not only a means of understanding the past, but is also an approach to social skills in the present, encouraging children to appreciate the feelings and attitudes of others, to work together, to share, discuss and develop ideas cooperatively.

Third hand comments long after the event have confirmed that children do recall their experience when they visit the house or castle again with parents or friends. We have certainly had instances of youngsters returning to one of the locations three years after the event to show their friends round and talk about what took place in the different rooms. This provides some confirmation that the projects really do increase interest in and respect for our historic heritage.

A particularly memorable example of craft work following the Bigod project was produced by a group of less able middle school pupils in the last two weeks of the term. They constructed a large model of a medieval village incorporating many details from the events at the castle, including representations of the trencher bread and the pens of sheep. It was remarkable for the standard of the work and the fact that it was completed on such a scale, indicating how strongly they have been motivated, and how much their research skills had developed.

Apart from the value to the children who take part, these projects contribute to the total of in-service training and curriculum development because they provide the inspiration, methodology and experience for smaller projects that are school based and organised by teachers themselves. The Advisory Service and Museum Education Service provide advice and help when asked, and assist with equipment and costumes from the items acquired for the major schemes. There have been several in-school historical drama projects in the county, and a greater appreciation of the value of linking history and drama has developed. It is interesting to see how some of these projects have led history and drama staff with colleagues from other departments (crafts in particular) to work together and pool their expertise in setting up such schemes with support from the Museum Service.

A professional tape/slide programme was made on each project to provide a permanent record and for use in future in-service training sessions for teachers. The photographer was suitably cloaked to conceal his camera and tape recorder so that he did not intrude on the scene that he was recording. He was able to capture many details of the events so that, after editing and making a linking commentary, we have extremely effective forty minute programmes, which have been shown to teachers' courses, parents' groups, professional organisations and general audiences. Recording the event is a great help in evaluating its impact.

While we have put forward these suggestions in the hope that others will find them useful, we shall continue to build on them ourselves in Suffolk. At Orford we are making the facilities available for a month for schools to mount their own projects with one class at a time, but supported by experienced group leaders. We are planning a reconstruction on a Roman theme, multi—cultural work and we continue to support a wide variety of school based projects in the county.

These major projects have involved us in working with at least one thousand five hundred pupils every summer for five years. In addition we have supported and observed many other projects set up by individual schools often using the equipment and the experience derived from the major reconstructions.

We hope that you will feel encouraged by reading about our experience to develop similar reconstructions.

BOOKS AND PUBLICATIONS

Appendix A.

Jane Austen *Mansfield Park* (First Published 1814)

Martyn Brown *One Museum's Drama Experiece* Museums Journal Vol 81 No.4.

Elizabeth Burton *The Georgians at Home* Arrow.

William Cobbett *Rural Rides* (First Published 1830) Penguin English Library

G. Ellis Burcaw *Can History Be Too Lively* Museums Journal Vol 80 no.1 (June 1980)

John Fairclough *Heveningham Hall Midsummer 1790* Museums Journal Vol 80 no.1. (June 1980)

John Fairclough *Heveningham and After* Journal of Education in Museums 3 (1982)

John Fairley *History Teaching Through Museums* Longman 1979

Henry Fielding *Tom Jones* (First Published 1749) Penguin English Library

Mark Girouard *Life in the English Country House* Yale University Press 1978

Molly Harrison *Children in History* Hulton

Charles Knightley *Bringing an Historic Environment to Life* Bulletin of Environmental Education (BEE) 85 (May 1978)

Dot. McCree *Drama and Heritage* Bulletin of Environmental Education (BEE) 85 (May 1978)

Philip Neal *Heritage Education* National Assn for Environmental Education 1979

Jo Newson *The Taste of Christmas Past* Times Educational Supplement. 21.12.84.

Thomas Peacock *Headlong Hall* (First published 1837) Dent

Richard Rabinowitz *Museum Education at Sturbridge Village* Museums Annual 1973 ICOM

Patrick Redsell *Heveningham Hall Midsummer 1790* Heritage Education News (Spring 1980)

Patrick Redsell *Learning About the Past* Outlook 20 National Assn of Drama in Education

A. Stevens *Dramatic Approaches to Museum Education* Journal of Education in Museums 2 (1981)

Teaching History Number 34 The Historical Association July 1982

Freeman Tilden *Interpreting Our Heritage* University of North Carolina 1957

SOME USEFUL SUPPLIERS AND SOURCES

Appendix B

Items	Supplier
Wooden Barrels Barrel Taps Wooden Buckets Adzes	Earthworks, 22 Corfe St., Ludlow, Shropshire. Tel. Ludlow 2010
Half Barrels Large Barrrels (Second Hand but very reasonably priced)	Leslie Watkinson, Paradise Farm, Brampton, Beccles, Suffolk. Tel. Brampton 229
Poles and Wood	Local Forestry Commission Office
Canvas & Cotton Twill Velour Wool Fabrics (Samples available)	J.D.McDougall Ltd., 4 McGrath Road, Stratford, London E15 4JP. Tel. 01-534 2921/1718
Hessian (Coloured) Muslin Flag Material (Casement)	B. Brown (Holborn) Ltd, Warriner House, 32-33 Greville St., London EC1N 8TD Tel. 01-242 4311
Replica Weapons and Armour (Hire)	Bapty and Co. Ltd., 703 Harrow Rd. London NW10. Tel. 01-969 6671
Costumes (Hire)	Bermans and Nathans Ltd., 40 Camden St., London NW1. Tel. 01-387 0999
Quills for Pens and Feathers.	Petits of Reedham, Camphill, Reedham, Norfolk. Tel. Reedham 243
Stone Masons (Students)	Dyfed College of Art, Carmarthen, Dyfed, Wales. Principal: J.G. Evans. Tel. Carmarthen 235855
Fabrics (Large range-good prices)	McCullock and Wallis, Derring St., off Oxford St. London. Tel. 01-629 0311
Wigs (Hire)	Wig Creations, 25 Portman Close, London W1. Tel. 01-406 0771
Clay Pots/Jugs/Bowls (Made to order, any design)	James Fearnley, The Homestead, Metfield, Harleston, Norfolk. Tel. Fressingfield 479.
Costume Source Books:	*Costume Cavalcade*: Henny Harald Hansen, Pub. Methuen (Good general background and detailed colour illustrations) *The Evolution of Fashion (Pattern and Cut 1066-1930)* Margot Hamilton Hill & Peter Bucknell pub. Batsford. (Excellent large format book with illustrations, details and most importantly patterns for making costumes.)

THE HUNTINGFIELD TIMES

Number 2   HEVENINGHAM FRIDAY JULY 1st. 1790.   Price Sixpence

ELECTION OF MEMBERS OF PARLIAMENT FOR THE COUNTY

To the Gentlemen, Clergy and Free-holders of the County of Suffolk. The supporters of Sir Gerard Vanneck are reminded that the Poll will open at 9 o'clock on Tuesday 29th of June at the Cross in Ipswich. They are asked to vote early. Several public houses have been booked, for them, their horses and carriages. Transport will be provided from all parts of the county for those who need it. Accommodation is booked for them at houses on the roads from all parts of the county to Ipswich.

from Sir Gerald Vanneck, Heveningham, 17th June, 1790.

God's Divine Order.

Speaking at Halesworth in connection with the forthcoming elections, Parson Williams spoke of man's duty to remain contentedly in the niches which had been appointed for them. A gentleman might seem to some of his listeners to have a pleasant easy life, compared to theirs at field labour; but he had duties and responsibilities far beyond their capabilities. He had to pay taxes, oversee his estate, and keep up his position by entertaining. The field labourer could not do these things, and nor did he suppose that a gentleman could cut as straight a furrow or thatch a rick as expertly as they could. The labourer should rejoice in his physical strength, and be thankful to the gentleman who found him work on his estate, and paid wages with his (the gentleman's) money.

HALESWORTH HOUSE OF INDUSTRY

Complaints have been heard of late that the paupers in the House of Industry at Halesworth are not well provided for in the way of food. The overseer has allowed this newspaper to print the details of two days' food which will show all fair minded men that the inhabitants are well nourished.

Monday:	Milk Pottage, Pease Soup Bread and Cheese.
Tuesday:	Rice, Milk, Salt Fish, and Potatoes Bread and Cheese.

SERVANT DISMISSED.

Elizabeth Cooper formerly a kitchen maid at HEVENINGHAM HALL, the home of Sir Joshua Vanneck has been found guilty of dishonestly removing quantities of tea from her employer, and of selling used tea leaves from the Hall to her neighbours in Huntingfield village. The defendant was imprisoned for one year, and will not be allowed to hold a position in service.

APPEAL TO THE PUBLIC

Being reduced from a state of affluence in which I lived in Ipswich for nearly 50 years to extreme poverty by unexpected events and a serious illness that prevented me working for 2 years, I ask with great reluctance for help to support myself and my numerous family. Those who wish to contribute to my relief can do so at the banking house of Messrs. Alexander, Cornwell & Co. in this town.

J. Dobson

On Wednesday June 30th will be held a Ball at the New Hall on the Quay at Ipswich. Tickets to be had at the Bath House at 3s. each. Tea, Coffee and Music included.

WANTED

William Houchell Labourer

Absconded about six weeks ago, leaving his wife and child in the charge of the Industry House in the town of Halesworth, in the County of Suffolk.

He is about five feet eight inches high, rather slender, lank hair, and of brown complexion. Whoever shall apprehend him and bring him to the overseer at Halesworth shall receive one guinea reward.

THE TROUBLESOME POOR.

Reports daily reach us from all parts of the country of groups of labouring people causing much trouble by rioting for food. Many honest people consider these persons to have been greatly agitated by the events in France, where daily many of the ruling classes have been put to death by cruel and barbaric methods employed by the barbarians who have risen up against their natural masters.

THE ADVANTAGES OF BATHING

Sir Joshua Vanneck the occupant of Heveningham Hall has shown his enthusiasm for the new fashion of regular baths. Although there will be no water supply piped into the Hall, his enjoyment of the public bathing facilities in London encourage him to want to continue this practice here in Suffolk. The villagers of Huntingfield will continue to carry their water in buckets from the village pump.

MILITIA FIELD DAY

The East Suffolk militia had a grand field day at Ipswich when the men went through their various movements in a way that delighted a large crowd. The Colonel's marquee was pitched in which the ladies and gentlemen were entertained with strawberries etc. Afterwards the privates were given beer. In the evening there was a very genteel ball and supper.

CLOCKS AND WATCHES repaired with haste and accomplishment at the house of MR. WILLIAM PEEK in the MARKET PLACE at HALESWORTH.

PARSON WOODFORDE'S DIARY

May 22nd, Friday ... I read Prayers this morning at Weston Church. My brother only walked to Church with me. It being exceeding cold and windy, the ladies did not go to Church from my house. Gave my Clerk, J^s Smith, a good black striped coat and waist-coat a p^r of Velveret Breeches and a powdered wig, this Afternoon at my house, and likewise a dinner of cold meat. Had a Note from Mr. Du Quesne this morning with a present of a score fine Smelts brought with him from Ely, he returned home yesterday. Gave the boy that brought the note 0.0.6. We had no meat for dinner today, but only some Smelts, boiled eggs, fritters and toasted cheese. I did not play at Quadrille this evening but my brother and wife, Mrs. Clarke and Nancy did till after 8 tonight.

May 23rd, Saturday ... It was very near 11 before we finished breakfast. My brother drove Mrs. Clarke out in my little Cart this morning on Sparham Heath. Nancy was very pert and saucy at dinner today. About tea time this evening Nunn Davy from Yoxford in Suffolk called here in his road to his mothers at Foulsham, and he drank tea, supped and slept here, he came on a little Hobby. At cards, Commerce, this evening lost 0.1.0. Nancy won both Pools, 6^d each person put in at a pool. Miss Custance still very bad in the Scarlet Fever.

May 24th Sunday ... Paid my servants their years wages this morn. To my Maid, Betty Dade £5.5.0. To my Man, Ben Leggatt £10.0.0. To my Man, Bretingham Scurl £8.0.0. To my Boy, John Dalliday £2.2.0. At Quadrille this evening lost £0.1.0.

May 25th, Monday ... Was taken very ill (this) morning in bed about 4 o'clock with a violent pain in my stomach, which I apprehend proceeded from gouty wind there and likewise from bile. I continued ill all the whole day, could not eat any dinner &c. In the afternoon was taken with a vomiting, and afterwards was some matter easier. I took a small Dose of Rhubard and Ginger going to bed tonight, as did my brother also. Pray God! I might be better to Morrow, as it adds to my uneasiness to make my Somersett Friends not enjoy themselves as well as I could wish. My poor old Clerk, J^s Smith is very ill, he dined with our Folks in Kitchen today but looks very bad. It was very wet this evening but quite warm.

A CAUTION TO BARLEY GLEANERS

I James Freeman of Bungay, Labourer, being today released from Bury Gaol where I was in prison because Sarah my wife gleaned barley off certain lands in Bungay, do sincerely thank the prosecutors and gentlemen who agreed to my release. I and my wife promise we will not be guilty of gleaning in future and ask that this notice appear at our expense as a warning to others.

The mark X of James Freeman
The mark X of Sarah Freeman

A VERY ELEGANT BALL

The new Hall at Heveningham was pronounced most elegant by guests who attended an occasion there this week. It has the essential minimum of three rooms. One for dancing, one for cards, and one for supper.

NEW CARPETS.

The English skill at invention has brought about the development of a new and cheap floor covering for use in houses. The new process involves the melting of pitch, beeswax, resin and linseed oil. This heated mixture is then rolled into canvas, and allowed to dry. The new floor covering can be cleaned by the application of milk, which is then polished until dry.

INSECTS OF SUMMER

Bugs and Fleas can be eased from their haunts in the beds and bed linen of sleeping rooms by a number of measures.

1. Set open the windows of bedchambers and uncover the beds to sweeten and air them.

2. Brush furnishings and furniture with a mixture of Wine, Camphor and Turpentine.

CAMPHIRE a most excellent preparation for the destruction of bugs and fleas to be found in bed linen and bedrooms may be purchased from the Halesworth shop of MR. PEEK lately opened in the MARKET PLACE. All manner of clocks and watches also repaired speedily and with efficiency.

TUTOR FOR THE VANNECK FAMILY

The children of Sir Joshua and Lady Maria Vanneck will be attended by a visiting tutor, who will school them from the age of eight in reading, writing, French, Italian and Music. The girls will be taught deportment. The children will be expected to address their mother and father as Madam and Sir. Manners are of the utmost importance in children believes Sir Joshua Vanneck. No plans are being made for the children of the servants working at the Hall to attend schooling.

SUMMER ICE

The domed building to be seen in the grounds of the Hall at Heveningham is the Ice House. A great pit some twenty feet under the earth has been dug, and lined with brick. The nearness of the lake to the Ice House will permit quantities of the frozen surface of the lake to be conveyed to the store throughout the winter, so that a plentiful supply of ice will be available through the summer.

WARNING TO TRESPASSERS

Great Trespasses have been committed in the woods of Giffords Hall Estate and on the fisheries of the manor. Notice is given that Samuel Ely is employed as gamekeeper to look after the woods, game and fisheries. Any person found killing the game or trespassing in any way or fishing in the fisheries after this notice will be prosecuted as the law directs.

CHANGE OF HEART

We are lately informed that the splendid entrance hall at Heveningham was, in fact re-designed before it was built. What was originally planned as a two storied building, the upper part being a gallery has now become a huge room, with no gallery, but with a vaulted ceiling. The walls and ceiling are in shades of green, with white details, while the floor is of rough stone and marble. Our readers may care to amuse themselves by speculating from whence the marble came, and how it was transported to the Hall. Sir Joshua Vanneck is to be complimented upon the beauty of this room in his house.

SCHOOL

Bury St. Edmunds Guildhall Street

Mrs. Steele thanks the friends of her school for their support and hopes to earn their future support. Her school will be open again on Monday July 19th. Terms are: under 12 years of age - Twelve guineas per year, at 12 and upwards Fourteen guineas and one guinea entrance.

MEALS FOR FASHIONABLE SOCIETY

Breakfast - about 10.00 - 11.00 a.m. or later if friends arrive. A light meal of bread or toast and butter with tea, coffee or chocolate. Toast is an English invention, which delights many foreigners, one of whom has suggested that it was invented because English houses are so cold in winter that the butter was too hard to spread easily unless the bread was toasted. Some prefer the traditional breakfast of bread and cheese with beer or cider.

Dinner - to be started between 3.00 and 5.00 p.m. Dinner in England lasts from four to five hours. Dinner shall generally consist of two courses, each being from three to nine meat dishes (such as a 20 to 30lb joint of beef or a whole side of mutton) and an equal number of side dishes. In England we do not have separate cooking for the servants, who join in all the courses eaten by the Masters. The Masters having first choice and the servants what remains.

In the country dinner is often served earlier. I have been served Sunday Dinner as soon as the family and guests return from morning service. Then comes a two hour gap between dinner and tea, but guests can still leave after tea, before it gets dark. The ladies may withdraw to the drawing room for an hour, before ordering tea and sending for the men to finish drinking and join them. Once the ladies have left the table men may discuss politics. They may also use the chamber pots which are concealed in the sideboard.

Afternoon tea is a way of rounding off dinner. It may take place any time between mid-afternoon and about half past eight in the evening, depending on the time and length of dinner.

Supper is generally served at about ten or eleven o'clock as a choice of cold meats, fruit and wine. On special occasions supper parties may include hot dishes and special sweets.

CRICKETING

The Gentlemen of the Huntingfield Cricket Club now wish to meet any eleven in the County of Suffolk for a match on August 10th. Please to direct letters to Mr. Fuller at Huntingfield. Stumps pitched at Eleven and Dinner at Two. For the benefit of Mr. Allen the Bath Keeper.

ARTIST AT HEVENINGHAM HALL

Sir Joshua Vanneck has engaged the famous Dutch artist Hertz VanRental to paint a series of pictures showing various aspects of the New Hall at Heveningham. We are also told that Sir Joshua may commission portraits of the whole Vanneck family.

Mr. VanRental and his apprentices are expected to start work this week.

ELECTION PREPARATIONS

Next Tuesday will see the election of members of Parliament for the County of Suffolk. The contest is expected to be a strong one. On Thursday the workmen began to erect the booths on the Cornhill in Ipswich, where the freeholders are to give their votes. There will be 15 booths for this purpose, so it is expected that the election will be over in two days.

UNADORNED NATURE

Mr. Lancelot "Capability" Brown has described his work on the Grounds of Heveningham Hall as The Simplicity of Unadorned Nature. He was aiming to match the house with the beauty of the surrounding countryside. A small hill has been removed by many men digging at it with spades, and a lake created to give a greater variety of nature around the house. Our readers will remember the great beauty of these grounds in the summer, with green lawns sweeping to the very door of the house, looking for all the world a vast green carpet, mown and cropped by Sir Joshua Vanneck's herds of sheep, and rolled by rollers drawn by horses, their hooves wrapped in woollen mufflers.

Thomas Swain. Razor Maker in BEDFORD STREET near Bedford Rowe makes all Sorts of Knives and Forks and Mounts Blades in Silver and Aggat and all other Sorts London.

IMPROVED KITCHEN

The kitchens at Heveningham will incorporate the most recent devices for the cooking and preparation of food. A clockwork spit has been provided above the kitchen range, and a fan in the chimney is turned by the hot air rising from the fire. Coal will be used as well as wood from the estate.

MEETINGS

IPSWICH RACES 1790 JULY 6, 7 AND 8

On Tuesday 6th July His Majesty's plate of 100 guineas will be run for on Ipswich Racecourse by any 4 year old horse, mare or gelding. No dogs will be allowed on the course. The public are asked not to go inside the ropes where the horses run.

COCK FIGHTING

Cockfights will take place at the Cock and Pye, Ipswich on Tuesday, Wednesday and Thursday in the Race Week. Suffolk against Essex. Cocks to be pitted at twelve o'clock on Tuesday and as soon as the race is over, and on Wednesday at ten o'clock and fight two pits before the race and on Thursday the same.

WANTED

Wanted immediately, a Journeyman Tallow Chandler who can come well recommended from his last place. For particulars, enquire of Mr. David Caddick Grocer and Tallow Chandler, Woolpit, Suffolk.

Kitchen Maid desired for work at Heveningham Hall. Must milk 3 or 4 cows, and know how to boil and roast fowls and butcher's meat. Washing day one each month. Must clean great stairs and scour kitchen irons as well as pewter in use. Must spin wool when work is done.

WANTED a youth of genius and good disposition not less than 17 years of age as an articled assistant in a school. Write direct (post paid) to William Harmer, Ipswich.

A BANQUET.

The Lord Mayor of London, giving a banquet in honour of his Majesty the King has called upon the Master Bakers of St. Pauls to produce a dessert. Information reaching us tells that the set piece is to be in the form of a cake, some twelve feet by seven feet, composed in the shape of a chariot surrounded by pyramids, triumphal arches and palm trees above four feet tall, all done in sugar, marzipan and sweetmeats. The Banquet is to be given on the evening of July 5th in London.

BREECHING

Although it is still common among the higher ranks to keep boys in long white frocks and sashes until the age of six or seven, many people now find it more convenient to breech their sons at three or four.

It is recommended that the boy be made a shirt like a man's except that the collar be large and frilled and worn outside the jacket. The jacket should be worn inside the trousers, the latter being well buttoned up. The trousers should reach to the ankle bone. It is recommended that the trousers have separate linings to ensure proper cleanliness.

ADVICE FOR THE YOUNG GENTLEMAN

Stockings should be of silk or cotton. Take care to have your stockings fit well, particularly in the feet. They should be tied smooth and fast but not too tight. Never be without clean, white gloves.

ENGLISH 'COUNTRY' FASHION

France is no longer the leader in matters of fashion. Woman's dress has now a more casual charm with the disappearance of the 'hoop'. Dresses now fall softly around the body, held in position by a wide sash, with a bow. Instead of an elaborate coiffure, the hair can now be worn in loose curls down the back. A 'fichu' or small scarf, worn around the shoulders and crossed on the breast completes this most elegant fashion, and worn with a large, broad-brimmed Italian straw hat would do justice to the natural beauty of the Englishwoman.

CHARACTERISTICS OF THE VULGAR

A new book lately published by Edgar and Sons, and Written by the Reverend Dr. Walker of Newbold in Yorkshire instructs the young not born or bred into good taste how they might achieve good manners. Those who wish to shed the characteristics of the vulgar should.

1. Learn that it is bad manners to put one's nose into the plate, or to eat too quickly or slowly.

2. That one must not when at table smell one's meat before placing it in the mouth.

3. That scratching, spitting or blowing the nose at table must be avoided.

4. A person should not pick his teeth before dishes are removed from the table.

Dr. Walkers book may be purchased from the Halesworth Bookship of MR. WILCOCK in the High Street.

OBITUARY JULY 1ST 1790

Sir Matthew Bedfield, who was taken by Our Lord on the 28th day of June 1790 at Bedfield Manor being 72 years of Age.

Mrs. Emma Hartling being the wife of the Rector of St. Marks at Cratfield who died during childbirth consumed with fever. The child being stillborn on the 6th day of June 1790.

Peter John Hall, his son James aged 2, his daughter Beth aged 7, his daughter Jane aged 8 and his son Peter aged 14 all being taken by the Smallpox during the month of June at Low Farm Ubbeston.

Benjamin Tollman Innkeeper of the Staging Post - The Royal Arms at Bungay - died of Consumption on the 3rd day of June 1790.

Miss Rachel Tompson who died during childbirth on the 17th day of June (the child surviving, being now placed in the Care of the House of Industry at Halesworth at the Parishes expense).

HUMBLE FOOD

A Dr. Perkins of Walpole having conducted a most comprehensive survey of the dietary habits of the population of England has concluded that amongst the poorer people of our land, Cheese, Bread and Tea are the basic foods taken. Most of our labouring classes would take beef only very seldom each year. Dr. Perkins who has lived and practised both in London and Suffolk condemns the practice of selling milk from open cans. This milk is transported from house to house by milkmaids walking from door to door. In Summer their cans of milk are covered in flies and dirt, the milk becomes sour and warm, and is unprotected from the deluge of slops thrown from the windows of houses in town.

THE SCOURGE OF EUROPE

A Doctor Ryder lately returned from travels in Europe has reported that eighty out of every hundred persons in our land can expect to contract the disease of smallpox, which he describes as the scourge of our times. While some are blinded, maimed and disfigured for life, many will escape with mild attacks which leave no ill effects. Dr. Ryder believes that the new device of innoculation, in which a vein of the patient is opened and a little of the venom let in, will rid us of the disease. In doing so, it will at once eliminate our towns from

those victims of the disease who being turned out of their houses now accost us and beg money from us.

TURNPIKE MEETING

For the Turnpike Road from Ipswich to South Town, Great Yarmouth and from that road at Beech Lane in Darsham to Bungay, there will be a meeting of the trustees at the Bell in Saxmundham on Wednesday 14th July at 11 o'clock.

1789

COACHES

Coaches will leave the Kings Head Norwich at 3 o'clock daily and can be expected to arrive at the Angel Inn Gt. Yarmouth at around 7 in the evening. Passengers are advised to book seats with the Coachman at a charge of 3s. Horses will be changed at Acle.

SAND CAUSES ILLNESS

Mrs. Davies the housekeeper at Heveningham, lately arrived from Bramford House in Ipswich, deplores the practice of scouring the inside of pans with sand to get them clean. She believes that this can cause great illness, and that scraping should be done with the finger nails. Mrs. Davies brings with her a new recipe for the making of soap which incorporates a mixture of ashes, lime and tallow, blended with oils from certain flowers in the garden.

THE NEW TRANSPORT

An improvement to our roads in Suffolk has made communication to Heveningham much easier. The speed of travel brings with it much danger however. It is said that a young man in a phaeton can now travel one hundred miles distant from London in a single weekend, and return to the capital to take up his business affairs by Monday morning. Many have refused to travel in the phaeton before their will is signed.

IMPROVEMENTS TO THE HOUSE

Gentlemen who wish to improve their houses with the latest inventions are fitting indoor water-closets to the design of Joseph Bramah patented in 1778. These provide a very satisfactory replacement for the outdoor earth-closets.

Wants a place immediately as a lady's maid. A well educated person; can work well with her needle, dress hair and has had the small pox. Letters, post paid, directed to AB to be left at the Post Office, Coddenham, where they will be duly attended to.

FOOLISH MEDICINES

A reputable physician has spoken out against many traditional cures for illness. Many of them he says are dangerous, others, merely foolish. In particular he speaks of swallowing nine lice each morning to cure jaundice. Using an application of hog's dung to stop bleeding. Tying a frog round the neck to cure nose bleeding. Pills made from cobwebs for the treatment of asthma. Readers who have been cured by these well known methods will treat the doctor's words with suspicion.

REMEDY FOR CONSUMPTION

A Mr. Hume reports that he has quite cured himself of consumption by the use of Snail Water taken each day. To make this, he roasts a good quantity of Snails, adding to them slit earth worms, and then leaving it to brew some time in a mixture of ale, herbs and a dozen other ingredients.

LABOURER WANTED to work on the HOME FARM AT HEVENINGHAM. WAGES £20 each year, breakfast and beer given free. Work in Harvest fields for labourers family may add £3.

Perch Phaeton, 1790

Produced for Heveningham Hall Midsummer 1790 A Suffolk Schools project. Project Team June Bowry, John Fairclough, Rory Kelsey, Patrick Redsell, from the Advisory Service. Paul Hobbs, Frances Nerini and Mick Richardson, from Lowestoft Theatre Centre.

BIGOD'S SUFFOLK 1173
A Manual for Apprentices.

Suffolk County Council Education Department

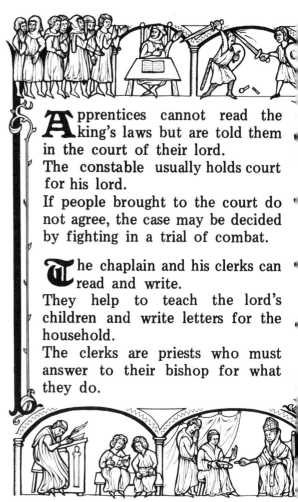

Apprentices cannot read the king's laws but are told them in the court of their lord.

The constable usually holds court for his lord.

If people brought to the court do not agree, the case may be decided by fighting in a trial of combat.

The chaplain and his clerks can read and write.

They help to teach the lord's children and write letters for the household.

The clerks are priests who must answer to their bishop for what they do.

Manual Compiled by: John Fairclough & Patrick Redsell
Layout & Illustration: M. J. Richardson

Apprentices learn from their master, with whom they work.

They show respect for their master, his lord, his lady and for the King's Majesty.

Apprentices dress properly for their work.

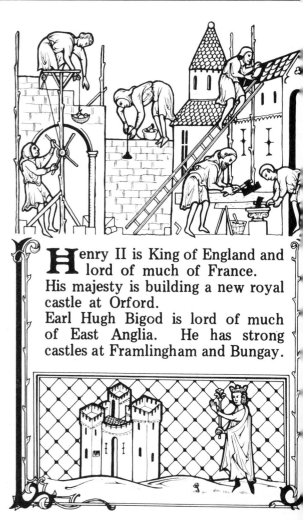

Henry II is King of England and lord of much of France.

His majesty is building a new royal castle at Orford.

Earl Hugh Bigod is lord of much of East Anglia. He has strong castles at Framlingham and Bungay.

The castle is the home of its lord and his family.

It houses his soldiers and twenty knights who owe him service.

Next in importance after the lord is the constable. He looks after the castle and its estates, keeps the accounts and receives taxes.

The chaplain prays for the lord and his household, keeps the lord's seal and writes his letters.

The marshal has charge of the stables, grooms and messengers.

The armourer makes and repairs weapons.

Food for the household is all grown on the lord's estates.

The bread is made by his bakers, butter and cheese are prepared by his cooks.

The animals are killed and cooked on open fires - roasted on spits, boiled in fleshpots or brazed on a grid iron.

Many different plants are used for flavouring food and drink and for medicines and dyes.

Apprentices must learn which these are, recognise different kinds of tree wood and know where the wood is used.

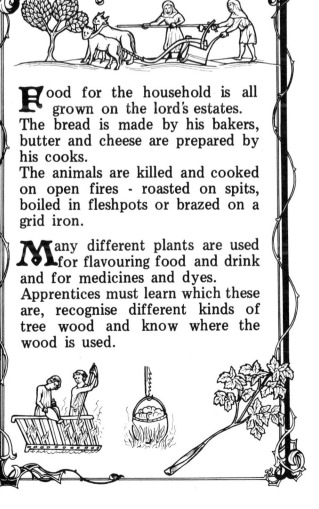

When the castle is under attack, the knights defend it.

Within the walls are stores and supplies in case of siege.

Attackers try to scale the walls with ladders and towers.

They catapult stones and spears at the castle from wooden machines and ram the gates to force their way in.

SERVANTS' COSTUMES

TURN YOUR COLLAR UP

WHITE NECKTIE

BLACK DRILL WAISTCOAT
(HIP LENGTH)

ROLL UP SHIRT SLEEVES

CUT OLD TROUSERS BELOW
KNEE AND ELASTICATE OR
TUCK THEM INTO LOCK SOCKS

DARK LONG SOCKS
(BLACK/GREY OR BLUE)

BLACK PLIMSOLES

MOBCAP
('FRILLS' LONGER AT BA

MUSLIN SHAWL

CROSSED OVER AT FRO
AND TUCKED INTO TOP O
APRON. POINT AT BACK

SLEEVES ROLLED UP

WHITE 'LAWN' APRON
(APRON TIES UNDER TH
BUST AND IS MID-CAL
LENGTH) (TIES AT BAC

IF SKIRTS WORN
IT SHOULD HANG FRO
BUSTLINE TO ANKLES
(PLAIN COTTON OR
VERY SMALL PRINT)

BOYS COSTUME
PROVIDED : BLACK OR BLUE DRILL WAISTCOAT
WHITE 'LAWN' NECKTIE

EXTRA TO ACHIEVE THE EFFECT
A LIGHT COLOURED OR WHITE SHIRT
DARK TROUSERS (NO JEANS!)
DARK OR WHITE LONG SOCKS
BLACK PLIMSOLES

WAISTCOAT: MAKE A PAPER PATTERN (ADJUST
TO SIZE) MAKE BACK LOOSE, WITH TIES
TO TIGHTEN TO FIT

CUT MATERIAL
36" X 36"

NECKTIE

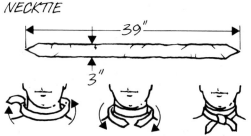

GIRLS' COSTUME
PROVIDED : A WHITE MOBCAP
WHITE MUSLIN 'SHAWL'
WHITE 'LAWN' APRON

EXTRA TO ACHIEVE THE EFFECT
A COTTON SKIRT OR LONG DRESS
AND BLOUSE

MOBCAP : AS PAPER PATTERN
PLACE ELASTIC NEARER FRONT
SO THAT 'FRILLS' OR GATHERS
ARE LONGER AT THE BACK

CUT MATERI
24" X 19"

BACK

APRON

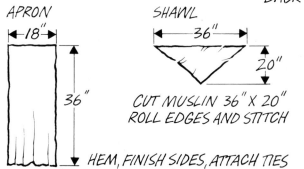

SHAWL

CUT MUSLIN 36" X 20"
ROLL EDGES AND STITCH

HEM, FINISH SIDES, ATTACH TIES

PRENTICES COSTUMES

NOTES: GIRLS HAIR - IF LONG, PLAIT IN ONE
PLAIT AT THE BACK OR TWO AT SIDES.
IF SHORT COVER WITH CALICO HEAD COVER.

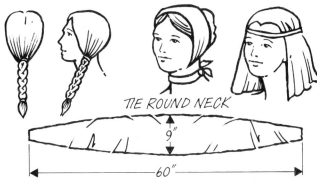

TIE ROUND NECK

9"

60"

BELTS: BOYS TO PROVIDE PLAIN LEATHER
BELTS. GIRLS' BELTS MADE FROM HESSIAN
AND CAN BE DECORATED WITH CROSS STITCH
IN WOOL.

IF ANY PUPIL WISHES TO ADD TO THEIR
COSTUME THEY COULD MAKE A COWL
COLLAR FROM CALICO TO WEAR ON
TOP OF TUNIC.

11"   8"

LEG COVERS:

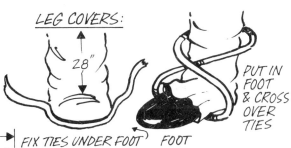

28"

PUT IN
FOOT
& CROSS
OVER
TIES

FIX TIES UNDER FOOT   FOOT

26"

← FLAT HEELS
OR MAKE
CLOTH COVERS

[BO]YS: TUNIC WORN OVER
[IN] TROUSERS (DARK - NOT
[JE]ANS!) WITH LEG COVERS
[TO] HIDE MOST OF TROUSERS
[AN]D SHOES.

GIRLS: LONG TUNIC WORN
WITH ROLLED UP SLEEVES
AND LONG BELT.
SANDALS ON FEET - NO
HIGH HEELS!

72"

28"   16"   28"

FOLD

CUT →

7" 8"

SLEEVE
EXTENSION

16"

7" 8"

20"

20"

20"

BOYS
TUNIC

GIRLS
LONG
TUNIC

48"

34"

TAKE IN HERE
IF NEEDED

60"

MAKE LEG TIES FROM HERE →

28"

18"   18"

LEG
COVERS

14"

1   2

JOIN

4" GIRLS BELT

2"

USING 72" WIDE HESSIAN -
CUT OUT TUNICS AS SHOWN
ON LEFT - ½" SEAM ALLOWANCE
NEATEN NECKLINES AND HEMS
BY HAND STITCHING RAW EDGES
TO INSIDE; OR USE EXTRA
MATERIAL AND FACE BACK;
OR USING THICK WOOL OVERSTITCH
THE EDGES (ESPECIALLY FOR
NECKLINES)
BOYS SLEEVES ARE SHORT BUT
GIRLS NEED SLEEVE EXTENSIONS

NEATEN IN SIDE SEAM
SO THAT SLEEVES CAN
BE ROLLED BACK.
TO MAKE LEG COVERS JOIN TWO
PIECES AND MAKE A TUBE
28" LONG. MAKE TIES 1½" × 70"
(OR 80") FROM SPARE MATERIAL.
NEATEN EDGES SO THAT IT
DOESN'T FRAY. FIX TIES UNDER
FOOT END (SEE ABOVE)
MACHINE BELT AND TURN
INSIDE OUT.

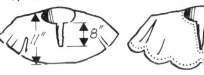

Acknowledgements

By their very nature, projects like *Heveningham Hall—Midsummer 1790* and *Bigod's Suffolk 1173* involve many people working together as a team. We cannot here name all the children and teachers who have been involved and from whom we have been able to learn and develop the ideas but we thank them for taking part with such enthusiasm, and for telling us how valuable and important this work has been in helping young people to understand the past.

We are particularly grateful to our County Education Officer, Duncan G. Graham and to Kenneth Johnson and John Underwood the Area Officers in Lowestoft and Ipswich; to June Bowry, formerly County Environmental Science Adviser for her help and advice; to Alison Heath and Mike Corbishley of English Heritage for their encouragement, to David Caddick, Julian Hilton and students from the University of East Anglia who have helped us to develop the use of role play; to Michael Richardson and Frances Nerini for inspiring and co-ordinating the design work; to Sandra Redsell and Martin Belville for preparation and organisation; to Kay Colman for supervising the administration; to Rory Kelsey and Paul Hobbs who found, made or built anything that was needed and finally to Stephen Wolfenden, whose outstanding photography has made an invaluable record of children working and learning at Heveningham and Orford.

John Fairclough
Patrick Redsell

Suffolk 1984